Breaking Free from Chronic Worry: A Guide to Taming Generalized Anxiety

Copyright Page

TITLE: Breaking Free from Chronic Worry: A Guide to Taming Generalized Anxiety

1ST Edition

Copyright @ 2023

ISBN: 9798223793830

Table of Contents

Breaking Free from Chronic Worry: A Guide to Taming Generalized Anxiety

By Roberto Miguel Rodriguez

Chapter 1: Understanding Anxiety Disorders

Definition and Types of Anxiety Disorders

Anxiety disorders are a common mental health condition that affects millions of people worldwide. This subchapter aims to provide a comprehensive understanding of anxiety disorders, including their definition and various types. By delving into these topics, the goal is to equip readers with the knowledge they need to identify and address their own struggles with anxiety.

Anxiety disorders are characterized by excessive, persistent worry or fear that significantly interferes with daily activities. While it is normal to experience occasional anxiety in certain situations, anxiety disorders are marked by the intensity and duration of these feelings. They can be debilitating, impacting relationships, work, and overall well-being.

There are several types of anxiety disorders, each with its own unique symptoms and triggers. Understanding these distinctions is crucial for developing effective coping strategies. Here are some of the most common anxiety disorders:

1. Generalized Anxiety Disorder (GAD): GAD is characterized by chronic and excessive worry about various aspects of life, such as work, health, and relationships. Individuals with GAD often struggle with controlling their worry and experience physical symptoms like restlessness, fatigue, and muscle tension.

2. Social Anxiety Disorder: Social anxiety disorder involves an intense fear of social situations and the scrutiny of others. People with this disorder may avoid social interactions, leading to feelings of isolation and low self-esteem.

3. Panic Disorder: Panic disorder is characterized by recurring panic attacks, sudden episodes of intense fear accompanied by physical symptoms like heart palpitations, shortness of breath, and dizziness. These attacks can occur unexpectedly, leading to a fear of future attacks and avoidance behaviors.

4. Post-Traumatic Stress Disorder (PTSD): PTSD develops after experiencing or witnessing a traumatic event. It is characterized by intrusive memories, nightmares, and hyperarousal. Individuals with PTSD may also avoid situations or triggers associated with the traumatic event.

5. Obsessive-Compulsive Disorder (OCD): OCD is characterized by intrusive thoughts (obsessions) and repetitive behaviors (compulsions) aimed at reducing anxiety. These rituals can consume significant amounts of time and interfere with daily functioning.

6. Other Anxiety Disorders: This subchapter will also touch upon other anxiety disorders, including health anxiety, separation anxiety, test anxiety, performance anxiety, and work-related anxiety.

By providing a clear definition and overview of the various anxiety disorders, this subchapter aims to empower readers to recognize and better understand their own experiences with anxiety. Armed with this knowledge, individuals can take the first step toward breaking free from chronic worry and anxiety, ultimately leading to improved mental well-being and a more fulfilling life.

Prevalence and Impact of Anxiety Disorders

Anxiety disorders are highly prevalent in today's society and can have a significant impact on the lives of those affected. This subchapter aims to provide an overview of the prevalence and impact of various anxiety disorders, helping the public gain a better understanding of these conditions and how they can be effectively managed.

Social anxiety is a common form of anxiety that involves an intense fear of social situations. Individuals with social anxiety may experience extreme self-consciousness, fear of judgment, and avoidance of social interactions. This can greatly impact their personal and professional lives, hindering their ability to form relationships and thrive in social settings.

Panic disorder is characterized by recurrent panic attacks, which are sudden episodes of intense fear and physical symptoms such as heart palpitations, shortness of breath, and dizziness. These attacks can be debilitating, leading to a constant fear of having future panic attacks and avoidance of certain situations or places.

Generalized anxiety disorder (GAD) is characterized by chronic and excessive worry about everyday life events and activities. Individuals with GAD often struggle to control their worrying, leading to restlessness, irritability, and difficulty concentrating. This constant state of anxiety can significantly impact their overall well-being and quality of life.

Performance anxiety is a specific form of anxiety that arises in situations where individuals feel they are being observed or evaluated. It commonly occurs in public speaking or performing, leading to intense fear, trembling, and difficulty performing to one's full potential.

Health anxiety involves excessive worry and fear about having a serious medical condition, despite reassurance from medical professionals. This can lead to frequent doctor visits, unnecessary medical tests, and a constant preoccupation with one's health.

Post-traumatic stress disorder (PTSD) can develop after experiencing or witnessing a traumatic event. Individuals with PTSD often experience intrusive thoughts, nightmares, and flashbacks, which can significantly impact their daily functioning and overall mental well-being.

Obsessive-compulsive disorder (OCD) is characterized by intrusive thoughts, images, or urges, as well as repetitive behaviors or rituals performed to alleviate anxiety. These obsessions and rituals can consume a significant amount of time and energy, affecting various aspects of an individual's life.

Separation anxiety involves excessive worry and fear about being apart from loved ones. This can manifest in children as separation anxiety disorder, causing significant distress when separated from their primary caregivers.

Test anxiety is a common form of anxiety experienced by students during exams or assessments. It can lead to physical symptoms such as sweating, rapid heartbeat, and difficulty concentrating, negatively impacting academic performance.

Work-related anxiety can arise from excessive stress and pressure in the workplace. This can manifest as generalized anxiety, panic attacks, or even burnout, significantly affecting job performance and overall well-being.

Understanding the prevalence and impact of these anxiety disorders is crucial for the public to recognize the signs and seek appropriate help. By addressing these conditions, individuals can learn effective coping strategies and techniques to manage their anxiety, leading to a better quality of life and improved overall mental health.

The Cycle of Chronic Worry and Anxiety

Chronic worry and anxiety can be debilitating, affecting various aspects of our lives and hindering our ability to function optimally. Understanding the cycle of chronic worry and anxiety is essential to breaking free from its grip. In this subchapter, we will explore the intricacies of this cycle and how it manifests in different anxiety disorders.

At its core, chronic worry and anxiety involve a continuous loop of negative thoughts and physical sensations. For individuals with social anxiety, the fear of being judged or humiliated in social situations triggers a cascade of worry and anxiety. Panic disorder, on the other hand, is characterized by recurrent panic attacks, intense bouts of fear and physical symptoms such as a racing heart, shortness of breath, and dizziness.

In the case of generalized anxiety disorder, chronic worry becomes a constant companion, infiltrating every aspect of life. Performance anxiety revolves around the fear of public speaking or performing, while health anxiety manifests as excessive worry about one's health conditions. PTSD arises from traumatic experiences, leading to persistent anxiety and fear. OCD is driven by intrusive thoughts and rituals, which perpetuate anxiety. Separation anxiety focuses on the fear of being apart from loved ones, and test anxiety arises during exams or assessments. Work-related anxiety, a prevalent issue in today's fast-paced world, stems from stress and anxiety in the workplace.

The cycle of chronic worry and anxiety begins with a trigger, whether it be a social situation, a traumatic memory, or an upcoming test. This trigger activates the body's stress response, releasing stress hormones and preparing us for fight or flight. However, in individuals with chronic worry and anxiety, this response becomes exaggerated and disproportionate to the actual threat.

As the stress response kicks in, negative thoughts flood the mind, fueling increased worry and anxiety. These thoughts further intensify the physical symptoms, creating a feedback loop that sustains the cycle. Over time, this cycle becomes ingrained and automatic, making it difficult to break free.

To tame chronic worry and anxiety, it is crucial to interrupt this cycle. This can be achieved through various strategies, such as cognitive-behavioral therapy, relaxation techniques, and lifestyle modifications. By challenging negative thoughts, learning to manage physical sensations, and implementing healthy coping mechanisms, individuals can regain control over their anxiety and break free from the cycle.

In conclusion, chronic worry and anxiety create a detrimental cycle that affects various anxiety disorders. By understanding this cycle and implementing effective strategies, individuals can overcome their anxiety and reclaim their lives. Whether it is social anxiety, panic disorder, generalized anxiety disorder, performance anxiety, health anxiety, PTSD, OCD, separation anxiety, test anxiety, or work-related anxiety, breaking free from chronic worry is possible.

Chapter 2: General Strategies for Taming Anxiety

Recognizing and Challenging Negative Thought Patterns

In our journey to breaking free from chronic worry and taming generalized anxiety, one of the most crucial steps is recognizing and challenging negative thought patterns. Our thoughts have a powerful impact on how we feel and behave, and negative thought patterns can fuel anxiety and keep us trapped in a cycle of worry.

For those of us with social anxiety, it's common to experience negative thoughts about how we're perceived by others. We may constantly worry about being judged or humiliated in social situations. By learning to recognize these negative thoughts, we can start challenging them. Are there any real evidence to support these thoughts? What are the alternative, more balanced perspectives? By questioning and reframing our thoughts, we can begin to alleviate social anxiety and regain confidence in social interactions.

Panic disorder is characterized by sudden and intense panic attacks. These attacks are often triggered by catastrophic thoughts and fears of losing control or dying. Recognizing these negative thought patterns is essential in managing panic attacks. By challenging the validity of these thoughts and reminding ourselves that panic attacks are not life-threatening, we can reduce their intensity and frequency.

Generalized anxiety disorder (GAD) is marked by chronic worry and excessive fear about various aspects of life. Those with GAD often have a tendency to catastrophize and imagine worst-case scenarios. By identifying these negative thought patterns and replacing them with more realistic and positive thoughts, we can break free from the grip of chronic worry and find greater peace of mind.

Performance anxiety can be paralyzing for those who have to speak or perform in public. Negative thoughts about failure, embarrassment, or being judged can intensify anxiety and hinder performance. By challenging these thoughts and focusing on positive self-talk and affirmations, we can overcome performance anxiety and unlock our full potential.

Health anxiety, characterized by excessive worry about health conditions, can be a distressing experience. Negative thoughts about catastrophic outcomes or misinterpreting normal bodily sensations can heighten anxiety levels. Recognizing these negative thought patterns and seeking accurate information can help to alleviate health anxiety and promote a healthier mindset.

Post-traumatic stress disorder (PTSD), obsessive-compulsive disorder (OCD), separation anxiety, test anxiety, and work-related anxiety all involve their specific thought patterns that contribute to anxiety. By recognizing and challenging these negative thoughts, we can address the underlying causes of anxiety and develop effective strategies for managing them.

In conclusion, recognizing and challenging negative thought patterns is a fundamental step in breaking free from chronic worry and taming generalized anxiety. By actively challenging these thoughts, seeking evidence to support them, and replacing them with more balanced and positive perspectives, we can regain control over our anxiety and live a more fulfilling life.

Relaxation Techniques and Stress Management

In today's fast-paced and demanding world, it's no surprise that many individuals experience high levels of stress and anxiety. Whether you find yourself constantly worrying about various aspects of your life or feel overwhelmed by social situations, it's important to develop effective relaxation techniques and stress management strategies to break free from chronic worry and anxiety.

This subchapter aims to provide you with a comprehensive guide on how to incorporate relaxation techniques into your daily routine and effectively manage stress. Regardless of whether you suffer from social anxiety, panic disorder, generalized anxiety disorder, performance anxiety, health anxiety, post-traumatic stress disorder (PTSD), obsessive-compulsive disorder (OCD), separation anxiety, test anxiety, or work-related anxiety, these strategies can be beneficial to anyone looking to reduce the impact of stress on their lives.

One of the most effective relaxation techniques is deep breathing exercises. By focusing on your breath and taking slow, deep breaths, you can activate your body's relaxation response and calm your mind. This technique can be practiced anywhere, anytime, making it a convenient tool for managing stress in various situations.

Another powerful relaxation technique is progressive muscle relaxation. This involves tensing and then releasing different muscle groups in your body, promoting a deep state of relaxation. By systematically working through your muscles, you can release tension and reduce the physical symptoms of stress.

In addition to these techniques, this subchapter will also explore mindfulness meditation, guided imagery, and other relaxation exercises that can help you relax, reduce anxiety, and improve your overall well-being.

Furthermore, stress management strategies will be discussed to help you cope with the demands of everyday life. This includes time management techniques, setting boundaries, practicing self-care, and seeking support from loved ones or professionals when needed.

By incorporating these relaxation techniques and stress management strategies into your life, you can regain control over your anxiety and worry. Breaking free from chronic worry is possible, and this subchapter will provide you with the necessary tools to tame your anxiety and live a more fulfilling and peaceful life.

Lifestyle Modifications for Anxiety Reduction

In today's fast-paced and demanding world, anxiety has become a common struggle for many individuals. Whether it's social anxiety, panic disorder, generalized anxiety disorder, performance anxiety, health anxiety, post-traumatic stress disorder, obsessive-compulsive disorder, separation anxiety, test anxiety, or work-related anxiety, finding effective ways to manage and reduce anxiety is essential for living a happier and more fulfilling life. This subchapter explores various lifestyle modifications that can help individuals in different niches of anxiety find relief and regain control over their lives.

One of the first lifestyle modifications to consider is exercise. Engaging in regular physical activity has been shown to release endorphins, the body's natural mood elevators, which can help reduce anxiety symptoms. Whether it's going for a jog, attending a yoga class, or taking a relaxing walk in nature, finding an exercise routine that suits your preferences and schedule can significantly contribute to anxiety reduction.

Another lifestyle modification to consider is maintaining a healthy diet. Certain foods, such as those high in sugar and caffeine, can exacerbate anxiety symptoms. Instead, incorporating foods rich in omega-3 fatty acids, magnesium, and antioxidants can have a calming effect on the body and mind. Additionally, drinking enough water and avoiding excessive alcohol consumption can help regulate mood and decrease anxiety levels.

Incorporating stress management techniques into your daily routine is another crucial aspect of anxiety reduction. This can include practicing mindfulness and meditation, deep breathing exercises, progressive muscle relaxation, or engaging in activities that promote relaxation, such as listening to calming music or taking a warm bath. Finding what works best for you and incorporating these practices into your daily life can significantly reduce anxiety levels.

Establishing a consistent sleep routine is also vital for anxiety reduction. Lack of sleep can heighten anxiety symptoms and make it difficult to cope with daily stressors. Creating a relaxing bedtime routine, keeping a regular sleep schedule, and creating a comfortable sleep environment can help improve the quality of sleep and reduce anxiety levels.

Lastly, social support is essential in managing anxiety. Connecting with others who may be going through similar experiences can provide a sense of understanding and validation. Joining support groups, seeking therapy, or talking to trusted friends and family members can alleviate feelings of isolation and provide valuable coping strategies.

In conclusion, by incorporating these lifestyle modifications into your daily routine, you can effectively reduce anxiety and take control of your life. Remember that everyone's journey is unique, and it may take time to find the strategies that work best for you. With patience, perseverance, and a commitment to self-care, you can break free from chronic worry and live a life filled with calmness and joy.

Chapter 3: Social Anxiety: Dealing with Anxiety in Social Situations

Understanding Social Anxiety Disorder

Social Anxiety Disorder, also known as Social Phobia, is a common mental health condition that affects millions of individuals worldwide. It is characterized by an intense fear of social situations, specifically those involving interaction with others. Individuals with social anxiety often experience overwhelming worry and anxiety about being judged, criticized, or embarrassed by others, leading them to avoid or endure such situations with immense distress.

This subchapter aims to provide a comprehensive understanding of Social Anxiety Disorder, shedding light on its causes, symptoms, and effective coping strategies. By addressing this topic, we hope to empower individuals struggling with social anxiety and their loved ones with the knowledge and tools needed to overcome this debilitating condition.

The chapter begins by exploring the origins of social anxiety, highlighting potential genetic, environmental, and psychological factors that contribute to its development. Understanding these underlying causes is crucial in order to address the root issues and provide effective treatment.

The subchapter then delves into the symptoms of social anxiety, which can manifest both physically and psychologically. Readers will gain insights into the various ways social anxiety can impact their lives, such as avoiding social situations, experiencing panic attacks, or constantly worrying about embarrassing themselves in public. By recognizing these signs, individuals can take the necessary steps towards seeking professional help and support.

Furthermore, this chapter offers practical strategies and techniques for managing social anxiety. From cognitive-behavioral therapy to relaxation exercises, readers will learn a range of evidence-based approaches that can help alleviate their symptoms and regain control over their lives. Additionally, self-help tips and real-life anecdotes from individuals who have successfully conquered social anxiety will provide inspiration and hope for those on their journey to recovery.

Lastly, this subchapter addresses the importance of seeking professional help and support for social anxiety. It emphasizes the role of therapists, counselors, and support groups in providing guidance, encouragement, and a safe space for individuals to share their experiences and learn from others.

By gaining a deeper understanding of Social Anxiety Disorder, individuals can begin to break free from its grip and lead fulfilling, anxiety-free lives. This subchapter serves as a valuable resource for the public, as well as individuals experiencing social anxiety and related niches such as panic disorder, generalized anxiety disorder, performance anxiety, health anxiety, post-traumatic stress disorder, obsessive-compulsive disorder, separation anxiety, test anxiety, and work-related anxiety.

Overcoming Fear of Judgment and Rejection

In today's society, it's not uncommon to struggle with fear of judgment and rejection. Whether it's in social situations, public speaking, or even at work, the fear of being judged or rejected can be paralyzing. This subchapter aims to provide practical strategies for overcoming this fear and reclaiming your confidence.

For those with social anxiety, the mere thought of being in a social setting can trigger intense fear and discomfort. The fear of being judged by others and the possibility of rejection can make it difficult to engage in conversations or attend social events. However, it's important to remember that everyone has insecurities and is more focused on themselves than on judging others. By challenging negative thoughts and gradually exposing yourself to social situations, you can desensitize yourself to the fear of judgment and rejection.

Panic disorder is characterized by recurring panic attacks, which can be triggered by fear of judgment or rejection. Understanding the underlying causes of panic attacks and learning relaxation techniques, such as deep breathing and progressive muscle relaxation, can help manage anxiety in these situations. It's also beneficial to challenge catastrophic thinking patterns and replace them with more realistic thoughts.

Generalized anxiety disorder is marked by chronic worrying, which often includes fears of being judged or rejected. Cognitive-behavioral therapy (CBT) can be highly effective in addressing these worries and changing negative thinking patterns. By identifying and challenging irrational beliefs, individuals can gain a more realistic perspective on social interactions and reduce anxiety.

Performance anxiety can be particularly challenging for those who need to speak or perform in front of others. Developing effective coping strategies, such as visualization, deep breathing, and positive self-talk, can significantly reduce anxiety in these situations. Seeking support from a therapist or joining a support group can also be beneficial in managing performance-related anxiety.

Health anxiety, post-traumatic stress disorder (PTSD), obsessive-compulsive disorder (OCD), separation anxiety, test anxiety, and work-related anxiety can all contribute to the fear of judgment and rejection. Addressing these specific anxiety disorders through therapy and other appropriate interventions will help individuals overcome their fear in these particular contexts.

Remember, overcoming the fear of judgment and rejection is a process that takes time and practice. By challenging negative thoughts, developing effective coping strategies, and seeking professional help when needed, individuals can break free from chronic worry and reclaim their confidence in social, professional, and personal realms. You are not alone in this journey, and with the right tools and support, you can overcome your fear and thrive.

Building Social Skills and Confidence

In today's fast-paced and interconnected world, social skills and confidence are crucial for personal and professional success. For individuals struggling with anxiety disorders such as social anxiety, panic disorder, generalized anxiety disorder, performance anxiety, health anxiety, post-traumatic stress disorder (PTSD), obsessive-compulsive disorder (OCD), separation anxiety, test anxiety, and work-related anxiety, developing these skills can be particularly challenging. However, with the right strategies and guidance, it is possible to overcome these obstacles and thrive in social situations.

This subchapter will provide practical tips and techniques to help individuals with anxiety disorders build social skills and confidence. It will address common fears and worries associated with various anxiety disorders and offer step-by-step approaches to tackle them effectively.

One of the key principles to remember is that practice makes perfect. Starting small and gradually exposing oneself to anxiety-provoking situations can help desensitize the fear response. Techniques such as systematic desensitization and exposure therapy will be explored, providing readers with a roadmap to face their fears in a controlled and supportive manner.

Additionally, the subchapter will delve into the importance of cognitive restructuring, which involves challenging and replacing negative and distorted thoughts with more realistic and positive ones. By identifying and reframing irrational beliefs, individuals can develop a healthier perspective on social interactions, enhancing their confidence and reducing anxiety.

The subchapter will also discuss the role of self-care in managing anxiety and building social skills. Strategies such as mindfulness, relaxation techniques, regular exercise, and proper sleep hygiene will be explored. These practices not only help regulate emotions but also improve overall well-being, enabling individuals to approach social situations with greater resilience.

Furthermore, the subchapter will address the importance of seeking support from mental health professionals, support groups, or trusted individuals. Therapies such as cognitive-behavioral therapy (CBT) and medication options may be considered, depending on the severity of the anxiety disorder.

By implementing the strategies outlined in this subchapter, individuals with anxiety disorders can gradually build their social skills and confidence. With persistence, patience, and a willingness to step outside of their comfort zones, they can break free from chronic worry and thrive in social and professional settings.

Chapter 4: Panic Disorder: Understanding and Managing Panic Attacks

Recognizing the Symptoms of Panic Attacks

Panic attacks can be incredibly frightening and overwhelming, leaving those who experience them feeling helpless and out of control. Understanding the symptoms of panic attacks is crucial in order to recognize them and seek appropriate help. This subchapter aims to provide a comprehensive overview of panic attack symptoms and equip individuals with the knowledge they need to identify and manage these episodes.

During a panic attack, individuals often experience a sudden and intense surge of fear or discomfort that reaches its peak within minutes. Physical symptoms commonly associated with panic attacks include a rapid heartbeat, shortness of breath, chest pain or discomfort, dizziness, trembling or shaking, sweating, and a feeling of choking or suffocation. Some individuals may also experience hot flashes or chills, nausea or stomach distress, numbness or tingling sensations, and a sense of impending doom or fear of losing control.

In addition to these physical symptoms, panic attacks can also manifest in various psychological and emotional ways. Individuals may feel detached from reality, experience intense fear of dying or going crazy, or have a strong urge to escape the situation they are in. It is important to note that panic attacks can occur unexpectedly or be triggered by certain situations or environments, such as crowded places or public speaking engagements.

Recognizing these symptoms is the first step toward effectively managing panic attacks. By understanding that these physical and psychological sensations are part of a panic attack, individuals can begin to develop coping strategies to regain control. Deep breathing exercises, grounding techniques, and positive self-talk can all help to alleviate the symptoms and prevent panic attacks from escalating.

For those living with social anxiety, panic disorder, generalized anxiety disorder, performance anxiety, health anxiety, post-traumatic stress disorder (PTSD), obsessive-compulsive disorder (OCD), separation anxiety, test anxiety, or work-related anxiety, recognizing the symptoms of panic attacks is particularly important. By being aware of these symptoms, individuals can seek appropriate support and treatment, such as therapy, medication, or self-help techniques tailored to their specific needs.

In conclusion, recognizing the symptoms of panic attacks is crucial for individuals dealing with various forms of anxiety. By understanding these symptoms, individuals can take proactive steps to manage their anxiety and seek the necessary support to lead a more fulfilling and worry-free life.

Coping Strategies During Panic Attacks

Panic attacks can be extremely distressing and overwhelming, but it is important to remember that there are effective coping strategies that can help you manage and reduce the intensity of these episodes. In this subchapter, we will explore various techniques that can be utilized during panic attacks to help individuals regain a sense of control and find relief from their symptoms.

One of the most effective coping strategies during a panic attack is focused breathing. By consciously directing your attention to your breath and taking slow, deep breaths, you can regulate your heart rate and reduce the feeling of suffocation or shortness of breath often associated with panic attacks. Practice inhaling deeply through your nose for a count of four, holding your breath for a count of four, and exhaling slowly through your mouth for a count of four. Repeat this pattern until you feel a sense of calmness.

Another technique is grounding. Panic attacks can make you feel disconnected from reality, so grounding yourself in the present moment can help. Focus on your immediate surroundings by naming objects you see or things you can touch. Engaging your senses through activities like squeezing a stress ball, smelling a calming essential oil, or listening to soothing music can also bring you back to the present moment.

Additionally, challenging negative thoughts can be beneficial. Panic attacks often trigger catastrophic thinking, leading individuals to believe something terrible is happening or they are in imminent danger. It can be helpful to question these thoughts and challenge their validity. Ask yourself if there is any evidence to support these thoughts and try to replace them with more rational and positive alternatives.

Incorporating relaxation techniques into your daily routine can also help reduce the frequency and intensity of panic attacks. Practices such as progressive muscle relaxation, guided imagery, and mindfulness meditation can promote a sense of overall calmness and relaxation, making you more resilient to stressors that can trigger panic attacks.

Remember, coping strategies may vary in effectiveness from person to person, so it is crucial to find what works best for you. Experiment with different techniques and be patient with yourself as you navigate through this process. With time and practice, you can develop a toolbox of coping strategies that will empower you to break free from chronic worry and manage panic attacks more effectively.

Long-term Management of Panic Disorder

Panic disorder is a debilitating condition characterized by recurring panic attacks, which are intense episodes of fear and anxiety. These attacks can be overwhelming and often occur without warning, making it difficult for individuals to manage their daily lives. However, with effective long-term management strategies, individuals with panic disorder can regain control over their lives and reduce the frequency and intensity of panic attacks.

One of the most important aspects of long-term management is understanding the nature of panic attacks. Panic attacks are not life-threatening, although they often feel like they are. Recognizing this fact can help individuals to challenge their anxious thoughts and reduce the fear associated with panic attacks. Education about panic disorder and its symptoms is crucial in building this understanding.

Another essential element of managing panic disorder is learning and practicing relaxation techniques. Deep breathing exercises, progressive muscle relaxation, and mindfulness meditation can all help individuals to calm their minds and bodies during a panic attack. By regularly incorporating these techniques into their daily routine, individuals can reduce their overall anxiety levels and be better prepared to handle panic attacks when they occur.

Cognitive-behavioral therapy (CBT) is a highly effective treatment for panic disorder. Through CBT, individuals can identify and challenge the negative thought patterns that contribute to their anxiety. They can learn to replace these thoughts with more realistic and positive ones, reducing the likelihood of panic attacks. CBT also helps individuals to gradually confront their fears through exposure therapy, enabling them to develop confidence in facing anxiety-provoking situations.

Medication can also play a role in the long-term management of panic disorder. Selective serotonin reuptake inhibitors (SSRIs) and benzodiazepines are commonly prescribed to reduce anxiety symptoms and prevent panic attacks. However, it is important to work closely with a healthcare professional to determine the most appropriate medication and dosage, as well as to monitor any potential side effects.

In addition to these strategies, adopting a healthy lifestyle can significantly contribute to long-term management. Regular exercise, a balanced diet, and sufficient sleep can all help to reduce anxiety levels and improve overall well-being. Avoiding caffeine and alcohol can also be beneficial, as these substances can trigger or exacerbate panic attacks.

Managing panic disorder is a journey that requires commitment and patience. By implementing these long-term management strategies, individuals can take control of their anxiety and lead fulfilling lives free from the constraints of panic attacks. Remember, seeking professional help and support from loved ones is essential throughout this process, as they can provide guidance and encouragement along the way.

Chapter 5: Generalized Anxiety Disorder: Coping with Chronic Worry and Anxiety

Understanding Generalized Anxiety Disorder (GAD)

Generalized Anxiety Disorder (GAD) is a common mental health condition characterized by excessive and persistent worry about everyday life events and situations. People with GAD often find it challenging to control their worries, which can interfere with their ability to function and enjoy life. This subchapter aims to provide a comprehensive understanding of GAD, its causes, symptoms, and available treatment options.

GAD affects people from all walks of life and can manifest differently in each individual. It is essential to differentiate between normal worry and GAD. While occasional worry is a natural response to stress, GAD involves excessive worry that is disproportionate to the situation at hand. This chronic worry can lead to physical symptoms such as restlessness, fatigue, muscle tension, and difficulty concentrating.

The exact causes of GAD are not fully understood, but a combination of genetic, environmental, and psychological factors is believed to contribute to its development. Individuals with a family history of anxiety disorders, a history of childhood trauma, or certain personality traits may be more prone to developing GAD.

Fortunately, GAD is a treatable condition, and various interventions can help individuals manage their anxiety and improve their quality of life. Cognitive-behavioral therapy (CBT) is an evidence-based approach that focuses on identifying and challenging negative thought patterns, as well as developing effective coping strategies. Medication, such as selective serotonin reuptake inhibitors (SSRIs), may also be prescribed in severe cases or when therapy alone is not sufficient.

In addition to seeking professional help, individuals with GAD can benefit from self-help strategies. These can include stress management techniques, such as relaxation exercises, mindfulness meditation, regular physical exercise, and maintaining a healthy lifestyle. It is also crucial for individuals with GAD to establish a support network and engage in activities they enjoy to help distract from excessive worrying.

By gaining a deeper understanding of GAD, individuals can recognize the signs and symptoms and seek appropriate help. This knowledge is especially valuable for those who experience anxiety in specific contexts, such as social situations, panic attacks, health concerns, or work-related stress. With the right support and strategies, it is possible to break free from chronic worry and lead a fulfilling life.

Cognitive-Behavioral Techniques for Managing Worry

Worry is a common experience for many people, but for those who suffer from chronic worry, it can become overwhelming and debilitating. Thankfully, there are effective techniques that can help manage and reduce worry. In this subchapter, we will explore cognitive-behavioral techniques specifically designed to tame generalized anxiety.

Cognitive-behavioral therapy (CBT) is a highly effective approach for managing worry and anxiety. It focuses on changing negative thought patterns and behaviors that contribute to excessive worry. One powerful technique used in CBT is cognitive restructuring. This involves identifying and challenging negative thoughts and replacing them with more realistic and positive ones. By recognizing and questioning the validity of our worry-inducing thoughts, we can gain perspective and reduce anxiety.

Another helpful technique is behavioral activation. This involves engaging in activities that bring joy and fulfillment, even when feeling anxious or worried. By participating in enjoyable activities, we can distract ourselves from worry and shift our focus to positive experiences. Additionally, relaxation techniques such as deep breathing, progressive muscle relaxation, and mindfulness can help calm the mind and body, reducing anxiety.

For those dealing with social anxiety, specific cognitive-behavioral techniques can be employed. These may include exposure therapy, where individuals gradually face feared social situations in a controlled and supportive environment, and social skills training, which helps individuals develop effective communication and social interaction skills.

Individuals struggling with panic disorder can benefit from techniques that target the fear of having panic attacks. This may involve gradual exposure to physical sensations associated with panic attacks, combined with relaxation techniques and cognitive restructuring to challenge catastrophic thoughts.

For those with generalized anxiety disorder, cognitive-behavioral techniques such as worry postponement and problem-solving skills can be effective. Worry postponement involves setting aside specific worry time during the day and postponing worries until that designated time. Problem-solving skills focus on identifying practical solutions to the issues that are causing worry.

Regardless of the specific type of anxiety, cognitive-behavioral techniques can be adapted to address the unique challenges faced by individuals with different anxiety disorders. The techniques discussed in this subchapter can also be applied to other anxiety-related niches such as performance anxiety, health anxiety, post-traumatic stress disorder, obsessive-compulsive disorder, separation anxiety, test anxiety, and work-related anxiety.

By utilizing cognitive-behavioral techniques, individuals can gain control over their worries and reduce anxiety. It is important to remember that managing worry takes practice and patience. With the help of cognitive-behavioral techniques and professional guidance, individuals can break free from chronic worry and live a more fulfilling and anxiety-free life.

Relaxation Exercises for GAD

In this subchapter, we will explore various relaxation exercises specifically designed to help individuals with Generalized Anxiety Disorder (GAD) find relief from chronic worry and anxiety. These exercises can also be beneficial for individuals facing other anxiety-related challenges such as social anxiety, panic disorder, health anxiety, post-traumatic stress disorder (PTSD), obsessive-compulsive disorder (OCD), separation anxiety, test anxiety, and work-related anxiety.

1. Deep Breathing: Deep breathing is a simple yet effective technique to induce relaxation. Find a quiet and comfortable place, close your eyes, and take a slow, deep breath in through your nose, allowing your abdomen to rise. Hold your breath for a few seconds, and then slowly exhale through your mouth. Repeat this process several times, focusing solely on your breath. Deep breathing helps calm the mind and promotes a sense of tranquility.

2. Progressive Muscle Relaxation: This exercise involves systematically tensing and releasing different muscle groups in the body to release tension and promote relaxation. Start by tensing the muscles in your feet, hold for a few seconds, and then release. Gradually work your way up through your legs, abdomen, arms, and all the way to your face. As you release each muscle group, focus on the sensation of relaxation washing over you.

3. Guided Imagery: Guided imagery is a powerful relaxation technique that involves visualizing calming and peaceful scenes. Find a quiet space, close your eyes, and imagine yourself in a serene location such as a beach, forest, or any place that brings you a sense of calmness. Engage your senses by visualizing the sights, sounds, smells, and even the sensation of the environment. Allow yourself to fully immerse in the experience and let go of any anxious thoughts.

4. Mindfulness Meditation: Mindfulness meditation involves bringing your attention to the present moment without judgment. Find a comfortable position, focus on your breath, and observe your thoughts and sensations without getting caught up in them. Whenever your mind wanders, gently bring your focus back to your breath. Mindfulness meditation helps cultivate a sense of calmness, awareness, and acceptance.

5. Relaxation through Movement: Engaging in physical activities such as yoga, Tai Chi, or gentle stretching can help release tension and promote relaxation. These practices combine movement with deep breathing and mindfulness, providing a holistic approach to relaxation.

By incorporating these relaxation exercises into your daily routine, you can effectively manage and reduce anxiety symptoms associated with GAD and other anxiety disorders. Remember, relaxation is a skill that requires practice, so be patient with yourself and make self-care a priority.

Chapter 6: Performance Anxiety: Overcoming Anxiety Related to Public Speaking or Performing

The Impact of Performance Anxiety

Performance anxiety is a common form of anxiety that affects individuals in various aspects of their lives, such as public speaking, performing, exams, and work-related situations. It can have a significant impact on a person's overall well-being and can hinder their ability to reach their full potential. Understanding and addressing performance anxiety is crucial for those who experience it, as it can greatly improve their quality of life and success in their chosen endeavors.

One of the most notable impacts of performance anxiety is the overwhelming feeling of fear and dread that individuals experience when faced with a performance or evaluation situation. This anxiety can manifest physically, with symptoms such as increased heart rate, sweating, trembling, and nausea. These physical symptoms can further intensify the anxiety and create a vicious cycle of fear and stress.

Performance anxiety can also have a detrimental effect on an individual's self-esteem and self-confidence. The fear of judgment and criticism can lead to a negative self-perception, causing individuals to doubt their abilities and talents. This lack of confidence can prevent them from fully engaging in their chosen activities and can even lead to avoidance behaviors to escape the anxiety-provoking situations altogether.

Furthermore, performance anxiety can hinder an individual's ability to concentrate and perform at their best. The intrusive thoughts and worries associated with anxiety can cloud their mind and impair their cognitive abilities, making it difficult to focus and recall information accurately. This can be particularly problematic in academic or work-related situations, where performance is evaluated and success is dependent on one's abilities to perform under pressure.

Fortunately, there are strategies and techniques that can help individuals overcome performance anxiety. These may include cognitive-behavioral therapy, relaxation techniques, visualization exercises, and exposure therapy. By addressing the underlying thoughts and beliefs that contribute to performance anxiety, individuals can learn to reframe their thinking and develop healthier coping mechanisms.

In conclusion, performance anxiety can have a significant impact on an individual's well-being and success in various areas of life. It is important for those who experience performance anxiety to understand its effects and seek appropriate help and support. With the right strategies and techniques, individuals can overcome performance anxiety and unlock their full potential in both personal and professional endeavors.

Techniques for Enhancing Confidence and Reducing Anxiety

Introduction:

In this subchapter, we will explore various techniques for enhancing confidence and reducing anxiety. These techniques are applicable to a wide range of anxiety disorders, including social anxiety, panic disorder, generalized anxiety disorder, performance anxiety, health anxiety, post-traumatic stress disorder (PTSD), obsessive-compulsive disorder (OCD), separation anxiety, test anxiety, and work-related anxiety. By implementing these strategies, individuals can regain control over their anxiety and build their confidence to lead a fulfilling life.

1. Cognitive Restructuring:

One effective technique is cognitive restructuring, which involves identifying and challenging negative thought patterns that contribute to anxiety. By replacing negative thoughts with more realistic and positive ones, individuals can reframe their perspectives and reduce anxiety.

2. Relaxation Techniques:

Practicing relaxation techniques such as deep breathing exercises, progressive muscle relaxation, and mindfulness meditation can help calm the mind and body. Regular practice of these techniques can reduce anxiety and enhance overall well-being.

3. Exposure Therapy:

For specific anxiety disorders like social anxiety, OCD, and phobias, exposure therapy is a highly effective technique. It involves gradually exposing oneself to feared situations or objects in a controlled and supportive environment, allowing individuals to confront their fears and gradually reduce anxiety.

4. Self-Care and Healthy Lifestyle:

Maintaining a healthy lifestyle plays a crucial role in managing anxiety. Regular exercise, sufficient sleep, a balanced diet, and avoiding excessive caffeine and alcohol can significantly reduce anxiety symptoms. Engaging in activities that bring joy and relaxation, such as hobbies, spending time with loved ones, and practicing self-compassion, can also boost confidence and reduce anxiety.

5. Seeking Professional Help:

While self-help techniques can be beneficial, it is important to seek professional help when anxiety becomes overwhelming or interferes with daily life. Therapies such as cognitive-behavioral therapy (CBT), medication, and support groups can provide additional tools and support in managing anxiety effectively.

Conclusion:

By implementing these techniques, individuals can develop the skills needed to enhance their confidence and reduce anxiety. It is important to remember that everyone's journey is unique, and it may take time and patience to find the strategies that work best for each individual. With dedication and perseverance, however, it is possible to break free from chronic worry and lead a fulfilling life.

Mental Preparation and Visualization Exercises

In this subchapter, we will explore the powerful techniques of mental preparation and visualization exercises that can help individuals tackle their chronic worries and anxieties. These techniques can be applied to a wide range of anxiety disorders, including social anxiety, panic disorder, generalized anxiety disorder, performance anxiety, health anxiety, post-traumatic stress disorder (PTSD), obsessive-compulsive disorder (OCD), separation anxiety, test anxiety, and work-related anxiety. By incorporating these exercises into your daily routine, you can take significant steps towards breaking free from chronic worry and managing your anxiety.

Mental preparation is a crucial aspect of anxiety management. By mentally rehearsing positive outcomes and envisioning yourself successfully navigating anxiety-provoking situations, you can build confidence and reduce anxiety levels. Visualization exercises involve creating mental images of calm and relaxation, replacing negative thoughts and fears with positive and empowering ones.

In this subchapter, we will guide you through various mental preparation and visualization exercises tailored to different anxiety disorders. For those dealing with social anxiety, we will offer techniques to help you feel more comfortable and confident in social situations. If you suffer from panic disorder, we will provide strategies to understand and manage panic attacks effectively. Individuals with generalized anxiety disorder can learn coping mechanisms to address chronic worry and anxiety.

Performance anxiety can be debilitating, but with visualization exercises, you can overcome your fears and enhance your public speaking or performing skills. Health anxiety sufferers will find techniques to address excessive worry about health conditions and regain control over their thoughts. We will explore how to manage anxiety stemming from traumatic experiences in individuals with post-traumatic stress disorder (PTSD).

For those dealing with obsessive-compulsive disorder (OCD), we will delve into visualization exercises to explore anxiety driven by intrusive thoughts and rituals. Separation anxiety can be challenging, but through mental preparation techniques, you can learn to handle anxiety related to being apart from loved ones. Test anxiety can be overwhelming, but strategies for managing anxiety during exams or assessments will be provided.

Finally, we will discuss coping mechanisms for work-related anxiety, helping individuals to deal with stress and anxiety in the workplace effectively. By addressing these various anxiety disorders and niches, we hope to empower you with the tools and techniques necessary to break free from chronic worry and anxiety.

In the following chapters, we will provide step-by-step instructions and practical exercises to help you implement these mental preparation and visualization techniques into your daily life. With dedication and practice, you can develop a mindset that is prepared to face anxiety head-on and live a life free from the constraints of chronic worry.

Chapter 7: Health Anxiety: Addressing Excessive Worry about Health Conditions

Understanding Health Anxiety (Hypochondria)

Health anxiety, also known as hypochondria, is a common form of anxiety that centers around excessive worry about health conditions. Individuals who experience health anxiety often find themselves preoccupied with thoughts of having a serious illness, despite having little or no medical evidence to support their concerns. This subchapter aims to provide an in-depth understanding of health anxiety and offer strategies for addressing excessive worry about health conditions.

Health anxiety can manifest in various ways, such as constantly checking for signs and symptoms, seeking reassurance from medical professionals, or avoiding situations that might trigger anxiety about health. It is important to note that health anxiety is not a form of malingering or seeking attention but rather a genuine experience of distress and fear.

The causes of health anxiety can be complex and may involve a combination of genetic, environmental, and psychological factors. Individuals with a history of anxiety disorders, traumatic experiences, or a family history of health anxiety may be more susceptible. Additionally, the widespread availability of medical information on the internet can contribute to heightened health concerns.

Addressing health anxiety requires a multifaceted approach that focuses on both the cognitive and behavioral aspects of the disorder. Cognitive-behavioral therapy (CBT) has proven to be an effective treatment for health anxiety. It involves challenging and reframing irrational thoughts, learning to tolerate uncertainty, and gradually confronting feared situations or triggers.

In addition to therapy, self-help strategies can be beneficial for managing health anxiety. These may include maintaining a healthy lifestyle with regular exercise, practicing relaxation techniques such as deep breathing or meditation, and engaging in activities that distract from health-related worries.

It is crucial for individuals with health anxiety to seek support from healthcare professionals who can provide reassurance and accurate medical information. Building a strong support network of friends and family who can offer understanding and encouragement is also essential.

By understanding the nature of health anxiety and implementing appropriate strategies, individuals can break free from the cycle of chronic worry and regain control over their lives. Remember, seeking help is a sign of strength, and with the right support, it is possible to overcome health anxiety and enjoy a fulfilling and anxiety-free life.

Managing Health Anxiety Triggers

Health anxiety, also known as illness anxiety disorder, is a condition that causes excessive worry and fear about having a serious medical condition. This subchapter aims to provide practical strategies for managing health anxiety triggers, helping individuals break free from chronic worry and regain control over their lives.

1. Understanding the Source of Anxiety: The first step in managing health anxiety triggers is to identify the underlying factors that contribute to these concerns. Exploring past experiences, family history, and personal beliefs about health can shed light on the origins of anxiety.

2. Education and Empowerment: Knowledge is power when it comes to managing health anxiety. Learning about common symptoms, medical conditions, and the likelihood of certain illnesses can help individuals differentiate between normal bodily sensations and signs of a serious health issue.

3. Develop Healthy Coping Mechanisms: Engaging in regular exercise, practicing relaxation techniques such as deep breathing or mindfulness, and maintaining a balanced diet can all play a crucial role in reducing anxiety levels. These coping mechanisms promote overall well-being and help individuals manage stress effectively.

4. Challenge Negative Thoughts: Health anxiety often stems from catastrophic thinking and irrational beliefs. Encourage individuals to challenge their negative thoughts by asking themselves evidence-based questions. Is there any concrete evidence to support their fear? What are the realistic probabilities of their concerns coming true?

5. Seek Support: Building a strong support system is essential for managing health anxiety triggers. Communicating with trusted friends, family members, or joining support groups can provide reassurance and help individuals gain perspective on their worries.

6. Limit Dr. Google: While the internet can be a valuable source of information, it can also fuel health anxiety. Encourage individuals to limit their online searches and consult with a healthcare professional instead. This will ensure accurate information and prevent unnecessary distress.

7. Cognitive Behavioral Therapy (CBT): CBT is a highly effective therapeutic approach for managing health anxiety. It helps individuals identify and challenge irrational thoughts, develop coping strategies, and gradually face their fears through exposure therapy.

8. Professional Help: In severe cases, seeking professional help from psychologists or psychiatrists who specialize in anxiety disorders can be beneficial. They can provide personalized treatment plans and support individuals in their journey to overcome health anxiety.

By implementing these strategies, individuals can regain control over their health anxiety triggers. Breaking free from chronic worry is possible, and with the right tools and support, individuals can lead fulfilling lives without being consumed by fear of illness. Remember, you are not alone, and there is help available every step of the way.

Seeking Appropriate Medical Help and Support

When it comes to managing chronic worry and anxiety, seeking appropriate medical help and support is crucial. While self-help strategies can be beneficial, sometimes professional assistance is necessary to effectively address the underlying causes and symptoms of anxiety disorders. This subchapter aims to guide individuals in finding the right medical help and support tailored to their specific needs.

For those struggling with social anxiety, panic disorder, generalized anxiety disorder, performance anxiety, health anxiety, post-traumatic stress disorder (PTSD), obsessive-compulsive disorder (OCD), separation anxiety, test anxiety, or work-related anxiety, reaching out for professional help is a vital step towards reclaiming control over their lives.

The first point of contact for seeking medical help is a primary care physician or general practitioner. They can conduct an initial assessment, provide a diagnosis, and offer treatment options. In some cases, they may refer individuals to a mental health specialist such as a psychiatrist, psychologist, or therapist who specializes in anxiety disorders.

Psychiatrists are medical doctors who can prescribe medication if necessary. They can evaluate the need for pharmacological interventions and monitor their effectiveness. Psychologists, on the other hand, use therapeutic techniques to help individuals manage their anxiety. They may employ cognitive-behavioral therapy (CBT), exposure therapy, or other evidence-based approaches to address the specific anxiety disorder.

Support groups can also be a valuable resource for individuals seeking help and understanding. These groups provide a safe space to share experiences, learn coping strategies, and receive encouragement from others facing similar challenges. Online forums and communities can be a convenient option for those who prefer anonymity or have limited access to in-person support groups.

It is important to remember that finding the right medical help and support may require some trial and error. Not every therapist or medication will be the perfect fit, and it may take time to find what works best. Patience and persistence are key during this process.

In conclusion, seeking appropriate medical help and support is crucial for individuals struggling with anxiety disorders. Primary care physicians, psychiatrists, psychologists, therapists, and support groups can all play essential roles in providing the necessary guidance and treatment options. Remember, reaching out for help is a sign of strength, and with the right support, it is possible to break free from chronic worry and tame generalized anxiety.

Chapter 8: Post-traumatic Stress Disorder (PTSD): Managing Anxiety Stemming from Traumatic Experiences

Understanding PTSD and Its Impact on Anxiety

Post-traumatic stress disorder (PTSD) is a mental health condition that can have a profound impact on an individual's life. It often arises in response to a traumatic event, such as a natural disaster, combat experience, sexual assault, or a serious accident. PTSD not only affects the person's emotional well-being but also has a significant impact on their overall anxiety levels.

PTSD is characterized by a range of symptoms, including intrusive thoughts, nightmares, flashbacks, and intense emotional distress when reminded of the traumatic event. These symptoms can be highly distressing and can lead to a heightened state of anxiety. Individuals with PTSD often experience a constant sense of fear and hypervigilance, always anticipating danger or the recurrence of the traumatic event.

The impact of PTSD on anxiety is far-reaching and can affect various aspects of an individual's life. One common area where anxiety is heightened is social situations. Social anxiety, a niche often experienced by individuals with PTSD, involves intense fear of being judged, embarrassed, or humiliated in social settings. This fear can lead to avoidance of social interactions, isolation, and a significant decline in quality of life.

Furthermore, individuals with PTSD may also experience panic attacks. Panic disorder, another niche connected to PTSD, is characterized by sudden and intense periods of fear or discomfort, often accompanied by physical symptoms such as heart palpitations, shortness of breath, and dizziness. These panic attacks can be triggered by reminders of the traumatic event or by situations that evoke feelings of fear or helplessness.

Generalized anxiety disorder (GAD), another niche related to PTSD, involves chronic worry and anxiety about various aspects of life. Individuals with GAD often experience excessive and uncontrollable worry about everyday events, such as work, relationships, health, and finances. The presence of PTSD can exacerbate these worries, making them more intense and pervasive.

Managing anxiety stemming from PTSD requires a comprehensive approach that addresses both the traumatic event and its emotional aftermath. This may involve therapy, such as cognitive-behavioral therapy (CBT), which helps individuals recognize and challenge negative thought patterns and develop coping mechanisms for anxiety. Medication may also be prescribed in some cases to alleviate symptoms.

It is crucial for individuals with PTSD to seek support and treatment to effectively manage their anxiety. By addressing the impact of PTSD on anxiety, individuals can regain control over their lives and work towards breaking free from chronic worry. Whether it is social anxiety, panic disorder, GAD, or any other niche related to anxiety, understanding PTSD and its influence is a crucial step towards healing and recovery.

Coping Strategies for Dealing with Traumatic Memories

Traumatic memories can be overwhelming, haunting, and can significantly impact our daily lives. Whether you have experienced a traumatic event yourself or know someone who has, it is important to understand that there are coping strategies that can help you navigate through these difficult memories. In this subchapter, we will explore various techniques and approaches to cope with traumatic memories and reclaim control over your life.

1. Seek professional help: Traumatic memories can be deeply ingrained, and it may be beneficial to work with a therapist specialized in trauma. They can provide a safe space for you to process and explore your emotions, helping you develop effective coping mechanisms.

2. Practice self-care: Engaging in activities that promote self-care can be a powerful tool in managing traumatic memories. This can include exercise, meditation, journaling, or spending time in nature. Find what brings you peace and make it a priority in your routine.

3. Connect with others: Isolation can intensify the impact of traumatic memories. Seek support from loved ones, join support groups, or consider participating in group therapy. Connecting with others who have experienced similar traumas can provide validation, empathy, and a sense of belonging.

4. Develop grounding techniques: Traumatic memories can make you feel disconnected from the present moment. Grounding techniques, such as deep breathing exercises, focusing on your senses, or repeating positive affirmations, can help bring you back to the present and alleviate distress.

5. Gradual exposure: Gradually confronting the memories associated with trauma can be an effective way to reduce their impact. Start with small steps, such as writing about the event or talking to a trusted friend. Over time, you can work towards more direct exposure, guided by a therapist.

6. Create a safety plan: Having a safety plan in place can provide a sense of security and control when traumatic memories resurface. Identify coping strategies, emergency contacts, and self-soothing techniques that you can turn to during challenging moments.

7. Practice self-compassion: Traumatic memories can evoke self-blame and guilt. Remember to be kind to yourself and practice self-compassion.

Remind yourself that you are not defined by your past, and healing takes time.

Remember, coping with traumatic memories is a unique journey, and what works for one person may not work for another. Be patient with yourself and seek professional guidance when needed. With time and resilience, you can break free from the overwhelming grip of traumatic memories and regain control over your life.

Seeking Professional Help for PTSD

Post-traumatic stress disorder (PTSD) can be an incredibly challenging condition to manage on your own. The symptoms of PTSD, such as intrusive thoughts, flashbacks, and intense anxiety, can greatly impact one's daily life and overall well-being. If you or someone you know is suffering from PTSD, it is important to seek professional help to effectively manage and overcome this condition.

Professional help for PTSD comes in various forms, including therapy and medication. One of the most effective forms of therapy for PTSD is trauma-focused therapy, such as cognitive-behavioral therapy (CBT) or eye movement desensitization and reprocessing (EMDR). These therapies help individuals process and reframe traumatic memories, reducing the intensity of associated emotions and symptoms. Therapists trained in trauma-focused therapies can guide individuals through the healing process and provide them with valuable coping skills.

In addition to therapy, medication can also be prescribed to alleviate the symptoms of PTSD. Antidepressant and anti-anxiety medications are commonly used to manage the anxiety, depression, and mood swings associated with PTSD. These medications can help stabilize emotions and reduce the intensity of symptoms, allowing individuals to engage more fully in therapy and other self-help strategies.

When seeking professional help for PTSD, it is crucial to find a therapist or psychiatrist who specializes in trauma and PTSD. These professionals have the expertise and experience to provide the most effective treatment tailored to your specific needs. You can start by contacting your primary care physician, who can refer you to an appropriate mental health professional. Additionally, there are numerous online directories and helplines dedicated to connecting individuals with mental health professionals specializing in PTSD.

Remember, seeking professional help for PTSD is not a sign of weakness but a courageous step towards healing and recovery. It is important to prioritize your mental health and well-being. With the support and guidance of trained professionals, you can develop effective coping strategies and reclaim your life from the grip of PTSD.

In conclusion, seeking professional help for PTSD is essential for effectively managing and overcoming this condition. Trauma-focused therapies and medications can provide valuable tools for healing and recovery. By reaching out to a therapist or psychiatrist specializing in trauma and PTSD, you can take the first step towards reclaiming your life and finding peace from the symptoms of PTSD. Remember, you are not alone in this journey, and professional help is available to support you every step of the way.

Chapter 9: Obsessive-Compulsive Disorder (OCD): Exploring Anxiety Driven by Intrusive Thoughts and Rituals

Understanding OCD and its Relationship to Anxiety

Obsessive-compulsive disorder (OCD) is a mental health condition characterized by the presence of intrusive thoughts, urges, or images known as obsessions, and the need to perform repetitive behaviors or rituals, known as compulsions, in response to these obsessions. OCD affects millions of people worldwide and can have a significant impact on daily life.

One important aspect to understand about OCD is its close relationship with anxiety. Anxiety is a natural response that helps us deal with potential threats or dangers. However, individuals with OCD experience anxiety that is excessive and out of proportion to the actual threat posed by their obsessions. This anxiety is what drives the compulsive behaviors as a way to temporarily relieve the distress caused by the obsessions.

For example, someone with OCD may have an obsession about contamination and feel intense anxiety at the thought of germs. To alleviate this anxiety, they engage in compulsive handwashing rituals, even though they may recognize that their fears are irrational. However, this temporary relief reinforces the connection between the obsession, anxiety, and compulsion, leading to a cycle that perpetuates the disorder.

Understanding the relationship between OCD and anxiety is crucial for effective treatment. In therapy, individuals with OCD learn to identify and challenge their irrational thoughts and develop healthier ways to cope with anxiety. Various evidence-based treatments, such as cognitive-behavioral therapy (CBT) and exposure and response prevention (ERP), have proven to be highly effective in managing OCD symptoms.

It is important for individuals struggling with OCD to seek professional help, as the disorder can significantly impact their quality of life. Therapists can provide guidance, support, and strategies tailored to their specific needs. Additionally, support groups and online communities can offer a sense of belonging and understanding, allowing individuals to share their experiences and learn from others who have faced similar challenges.

By understanding OCD and its relationship to anxiety, individuals can gain insight into their symptoms and take the necessary steps towards managing their condition. With proper treatment and support, it is possible to break free from the cycle of obsessions and compulsions, leading to a better quality of life and improved overall well-being.

This subchapter aims to provide a comprehensive overview of OCD and its relationship to anxiety, offering valuable information and resources for individuals struggling with OCD, as well as those interested in understanding the disorder and supporting their loved ones.

Cognitive-Behavioral Techniques for Managing OCD

Obsessive-compulsive disorder (OCD) is a mental health condition characterized by intrusive thoughts and repetitive behaviors or rituals. It can significantly impact a person's daily life and relationships. However, there are effective techniques that can help individuals manage their OCD symptoms and improve their overall well-being.

Cognitive-behavioral therapy (CBT) is a widely recognized and evidence-based approach for treating OCD. It focuses on challenging and changing negative thoughts and behaviors that contribute to anxiety and distress. Here are some cognitive-behavioral techniques that can be helpful in managing OCD:

1. Exposure and Response Prevention (ERP): This technique involves gradually exposing oneself to situations or thoughts that trigger obsessions, while resisting the urge to engage in compulsive behaviors. By facing their fears and resisting the compulsion, individuals can learn that their anxiety decreases over time, leading to a reduction in OCD symptoms.

2. Cognitive Restructuring: This technique aims to identify and challenge irrational thoughts or beliefs that contribute to OCD. By questioning the validity of these thoughts and replacing them with more realistic and positive ones, individuals can reduce their anxiety and break free from obsessive thinking patterns.

3. Mindfulness Meditation: Mindfulness involves focusing one's attention on the present moment without judgment. It can help individuals with OCD become more aware of their thoughts and emotions without getting caught up in them. By practicing mindfulness regularly, individuals can develop a greater sense of control over their thoughts and reduce the impact of OCD symptoms.

4. Thought Stopping: This technique involves interrupting intrusive thoughts by mentally shouting "stop" or using a physical gesture like snapping a rubber band on the wrist. By disrupting the obsessive thought pattern, individuals can gain a sense of control and reduce the intensity of their obsessions.

5. Self-Care and Stress Management: Engaging in activities that promote relaxation and self-care can help individuals manage their OCD symptoms. Regular exercise, adequate sleep, and healthy coping mechanisms such as deep breathing exercises or journaling can help reduce anxiety and promote overall well-being.

It is important to note that managing OCD often requires professional guidance from a therapist experienced in treating OCD. They can provide personalized strategies and support to help individuals navigate their specific challenges.

By utilizing these cognitive-behavioral techniques, individuals with OCD can gain greater control over their symptoms and live a more fulfilling life. Remember, it is possible to break free from the grip of OCD and find relief from intrusive thoughts and rituals.

Exposure and Response Prevention Therapy

Exposure and Response Prevention Therapy (ERP) is a powerful and evidence-based treatment approach used to effectively manage and overcome various anxiety disorders. Whether you suffer from social anxiety, panic disorder, generalized anxiety disorder, performance anxiety, health anxiety, post-traumatic stress disorder (PTSD), obsessive-compulsive disorder (OCD), separation anxiety, test anxiety, or work-related anxiety, ERP can be a valuable tool in your journey towards a more fulfilling and worry-free life.

At its core, ERP aims to challenge and disrupt the anxiety-provoking patterns of thoughts, emotions, and behaviors that contribute to your anxiety disorder. The therapy involves gradually exposing yourself to the situations, objects, or thoughts that trigger your anxiety, while simultaneously resisting the urge to engage in your typical anxiety-driven responses or rituals.

For example, if you struggle with social anxiety and fear public speaking, ERP would involve gradually exposing yourself to speaking in front of others while resisting the urge to avoid or escape the situation. Over time, this exposure allows you to confront your fears and learn that the perceived threats are often exaggerated or unfounded. By repeatedly facing your anxieties without engaging in the usual anxious behaviors, you can retrain your brain to respond differently and ultimately reduce the power of anxiety over your life.

ERP is typically conducted under the guidance of a trained therapist, who will work closely with you to create a personalized treatment plan tailored to your specific anxiety triggers and goals. The therapist will provide support, guidance, and encouragement throughout the process, helping you to gradually increase your exposure levels as you become more comfortable and confident.

Research has consistently shown that ERP is highly effective in reducing anxiety symptoms and improving overall quality of life. It empowers individuals to confront their fears head-on and develop healthier coping mechanisms, ultimately leading to long-term anxiety relief.

If you are ready to break free from the grips of chronic worry and anxiety, consider exploring Exposure and Response Prevention Therapy. Reach out to a qualified mental health professional who specializes in anxiety disorders to discuss how ERP can be incorporated into your treatment plan. Remember, you have the power to take control of your anxiety and live a life free from constant worry.

Chapter 10: Separation Anxiety: Handling Anxiety Related to Being Apart from Loved Ones

Understanding Separation Anxiety in Adults

Separation anxiety is commonly associated with children, but it can also affect adults. When individuals experience separation anxiety, they feel intense distress and fear when they are separated from their loved ones or familiar environments. This subchapter aims to shed light on the phenomenon of separation anxiety in adults and provide guidance on how to handle these distressing emotions.

Adults with separation anxiety often experience overwhelming worry about the well-being of their loved ones, especially when they are apart. They may constantly fear that something terrible will happen to their loved ones, leading to a heightened level of anxiety and distress. This anxiety can significantly impact their daily functioning, relationships, and overall quality of life.

Understanding the underlying causes of separation anxiety is crucial to managing and overcoming this condition. In many cases, separation anxiety can stem from past traumatic experiences or unresolved attachment issues. Additionally, major life changes such as moving, divorce, or the loss of a loved one can trigger separation anxiety in adults. By identifying the root causes, individuals can begin to address and manage their anxiety effectively.

This subchapter offers practical strategies and techniques to help individuals cope with separation anxiety. It emphasizes the importance of self-care, stress management, and building a support system. Exploring relaxation techniques, such as deep breathing exercises or mindfulness meditation, can also be beneficial in reducing anxiety symptoms.

Furthermore, cognitive-behavioral therapy (CBT) is often recommended as an effective treatment for separation anxiety in adults. CBT helps individuals identify and challenge irrational thoughts and beliefs that contribute to their anxiety. It also assists in developing healthy coping mechanisms and gradually exposing individuals to situations that trigger their anxiety, allowing them to build resilience and tolerance.

Throughout this subchapter, personal anecdotes and success stories from individuals who have overcome separation anxiety will be shared to inspire hope and provide reassurance to readers. Understanding that they are not alone in their struggles can be incredibly reassuring for individuals experiencing separation anxiety.

By providing a comprehensive understanding of separation anxiety in adults and offering practical strategies for managing and overcoming it, this subchapter aims to empower readers to break free from the grip of chronic worry and anxiety, providing them with the tools they need to lead a happier, more fulfilling life.

Developing Coping Mechanisms for Separation Anxiety

Separation anxiety is a common form of anxiety that many people experience when they are away from their loved ones or familiar environments. It can be particularly challenging to deal with, as it often leads to feelings of distress, fear, and worry. However, with the right coping mechanisms, it is possible to overcome separation anxiety and lead a more fulfilling life.

One effective way to manage separation anxiety is to gradually expose yourself to situations that trigger your anxiety. Start by spending short periods apart from your loved ones and gradually increase the time as you become more comfortable. This process, known as systematic desensitization, helps to desensitize your mind and body to the anxiety-inducing stimuli.

Another useful coping mechanism is to practice relaxation techniques. Deep breathing exercises, meditation, and progressive muscle relaxation can help calm your mind and body during separation. These techniques can be especially helpful when you are feeling overwhelmed or anxious.

Creating a support system is crucial when dealing with separation anxiety. Reach out to friends, family, or support groups who can provide understanding and encouragement. Sharing your feelings and experiences with others who have gone through similar situations can be incredibly comforting and empowering.

It is also important to challenge negative thoughts and replace them with more positive and realistic ones. Separation anxiety often stems from irrational fears and catastrophic thinking. By identifying and questioning these thoughts, you can gain a more balanced perspective and reduce your anxiety levels.

Engaging in self-care activities can significantly alleviate separation anxiety. Prioritize activities that bring you joy and relaxation, such as exercise, hobbies, or spending time in nature. Taking care of your physical and emotional well-being will enhance your resilience and ability to cope with separation.

Lastly, seeking professional help is always an option. Therapists and counselors specializing in anxiety disorders can provide invaluable guidance and support. They can help you uncover the root causes of your separation anxiety and develop personalized coping strategies.

Remember, overcoming separation anxiety takes time and effort. Be patient with yourself and celebrate even the smallest victories along the way. With the right coping mechanisms and support, you can break free from the grip of separation anxiety and lead a more fulfilling and anxiety-free life.

Building Healthy Relationships and Independence

In our journey to break free from chronic worry and anxiety, it is essential to focus on building healthy relationships and independence. Developing strong connections with others and fostering a sense of autonomy can significantly contribute to our overall well-being and help alleviate anxiety symptoms. This subchapter aims to guide you through strategies and techniques that can enhance your social interactions, strengthen your support network, and empower you to embrace independence.

Social anxiety can be a significant hurdle for many individuals, making social situations overwhelming and uncomfortable. We will delve into practical tips for managing social anxiety, such as gradual exposure and cognitive-behavioral techniques, to help you gradually conquer your fears and build confidence in social settings.

For those struggling with panic disorder, understanding and managing panic attacks is crucial. We will explore relaxation exercises, breathing techniques, and cognitive restructuring methods to help you regain control during panic episodes. Additionally, we will discuss the importance of seeking professional help and the potential benefits of medication in managing panic disorder symptoms.

Generalized anxiety disorder often leads to chronic worry and a constant state of anxiety. We will provide coping strategies, such as mindfulness meditation, journaling, and challenging negative thoughts, to help you regain a sense of calm and reduce excessive worry. Moreover, we will emphasize the significance of self-care practices, including exercise, proper sleep routines, and healthy lifestyle choices.

Performance anxiety can hinder personal and professional growth, causing distress during public speaking or performing. We will explore techniques like visualization, positive self-talk, and relaxation exercises to help you overcome anxiety in these situations. Additionally, we will discuss the benefits of seeking support from professionals, such as therapists or coaches, who specialize in performance anxiety.

Other anxiety niches, such as health anxiety, post-traumatic stress disorder (PTSD), obsessive-compulsive disorder (OCD), separation anxiety, test anxiety, and work-related anxiety, will also be addressed in this subchapter. We will provide specific strategies tailored to each niche, empowering you to manage anxiety symptoms effectively.

By building healthy relationships and fostering independence, we can cultivate a strong support system while developing the skills and confidence to navigate anxiety-inducing situations. Remember, breaking free from chronic worry is a journey, but with the right tools and support, you can regain control of your life and find peace and fulfillment.

Chapter 11: Test Anxiety: Strategies for Managing Anxiety during Exams or Assessments

Recognizing the Impact of Test Anxiety

Test anxiety is a common phenomenon that affects individuals from various walks of life. Whether you are a student, a professional taking certification exams, or someone taking an important assessment, the pressure to perform well can trigger overwhelming anxiety. In this subchapter, we will delve into the impact of test anxiety and explore effective strategies for managing it.

Test anxiety can manifest in several ways, including physical symptoms such as a racing heart, sweating, nausea, and difficulty breathing. It can also lead to cognitive symptoms like racing thoughts, negative self-talk, and an inability to concentrate. These symptoms can significantly hinder performance and impede one's ability to demonstrate their true abilities and knowledge.

The impact of test anxiety goes beyond the immediate stress experienced during exams. It can lead to a vicious cycle of self-doubt and fear surrounding future assessments, perpetuating a chronic state of worry. Moreover, individuals with test anxiety may avoid studying or preparing for tests altogether due to the fear of failure, further exacerbating their anxiety.

Fortunately, there are several strategies that can help individuals manage test anxiety effectively. One key approach is implementing relaxation techniques, such as deep breathing exercises, progressive muscle relaxation, and mindfulness meditation. These techniques can help calm the mind and body, reducing anxiety symptoms and improving focus.

Another helpful strategy is to develop effective study habits and time management skills. By creating a structured study plan and breaking down the content into manageable chunks, individuals can reduce the feeling of being overwhelmed and increase confidence in their preparation. Additionally, practicing self-care, such as getting enough sleep, eating well, and engaging in regular physical exercise, can have a significant positive impact on anxiety levels.

Cognitive-behavioral techniques can also be beneficial in managing test anxiety. Identifying and challenging negative thoughts related to performance and replacing them with positive affirmations can help individuals reframe their mindset and reduce anxiety. Seeking support from a therapist or counselor who specializes in anxiety can provide additional guidance and support in developing coping mechanisms specific to test anxiety.

Recognizing the impact of test anxiety is crucial for individuals to take proactive steps towards managing it effectively. By implementing relaxation techniques, developing effective study habits, practicing self-care, and utilizing cognitive-behavioral techniques, individuals can break free from the shackles of test anxiety and perform to their true potential. Remember, test anxiety is a common challenge, and with the right tools and support, it can be overcome.

Preparing Mentally and Physically for Tests

Tests can be a significant source of stress and anxiety for many individuals. Whether you are a student preparing for an exam or a professional facing a work-related assessment, the pressure to perform well can feel overwhelming. However, with the right strategies, you can effectively manage test anxiety and improve your performance. This chapter will provide you with practical tips to prepare both mentally and physically for tests, helping you break free from chronic worry and anxiety.

Mental preparation is key when it comes to facing tests. One effective strategy is to develop a study plan that includes regular breaks and allows for sufficient rest. Adequate sleep is crucial for cognitive function and memory consolidation, so make sure to prioritize a good night's sleep before the test. Additionally, practicing relaxation techniques such as deep breathing, mindfulness, or meditation can help calm your mind and reduce anxiety levels. Visualizing success and positive outcomes can also boost your confidence and alleviate test-related worries.

Physical preparation is equally important. Engaging in regular exercise not only improves overall well-being but also helps to reduce stress and anxiety. Physical activity releases endorphins, which are natural mood boosters. It is also essential to maintain a healthy diet, as certain foods like fruits, vegetables, and whole grains can provide the necessary nutrients for optimal brain function. Avoiding excessive caffeine and sugary snacks is also advisable, as they can increase anxiety and interfere with concentration.

Furthermore, adopting effective study techniques can enhance your performance and reduce anxiety during the test. Break down the material into manageable chunks and create a study schedule that allows for regular review. Practice active learning methods, such as summarizing information in your own words or teaching the material to someone else. Utilize mnemonic devices, flashcards, or other memory aids to improve retention. Finally, don't forget to simulate test conditions during your study sessions by practicing timed exercises or taking practice tests. This will familiarize you with the test format and help build confidence.

By employing these strategies, you can better prepare yourself mentally and physically for tests, reducing anxiety and improving your overall performance. Remember that everyone experiences some level of test anxiety, and it is normal to feel nervous. However, with proper preparation and self-care, you can overcome these challenges and perform to the best of your abilities.

Coping Techniques to Reduce Test Anxiety

Test anxiety is a common issue that many individuals, including students of all ages and professionals, face when it comes to exams or assessments. The pressure to perform well can lead to feelings of stress, worry, and nervousness, which can negatively impact performance. However, there are several coping techniques that can help reduce test anxiety and improve overall test-taking experience.

1. Preparation is Key: One of the most effective ways to combat test anxiety is by being well-prepared. Create a study schedule and stick to it, allowing yourself enough time to review the material thoroughly. Break down the content into manageable chunks and utilize different study techniques that work best for you, such as flashcards, mnemonic devices, or group study sessions.

2. Practice Relaxation Techniques: Incorporating relaxation techniques into your test preparation routine can significantly reduce anxiety. Deep breathing exercises, progressive muscle relaxation, and mindfulness meditation can help calm your mind and body. Practice these techniques regularly to build resilience to anxiety over time.

3. Positive Self-Talk: Replace negative thoughts and self-doubt with positive affirmations. Remind yourself of your past successes, and focus on your strengths and abilities. Encourage yourself with statements like, "I am well-prepared and capable of doing my best."

4. Visualize Success: Use the power of visualization to imagine yourself successfully completing the test. Picture yourself feeling confident, calm, and performing well. Visualizing success can help boost your self-confidence and alleviate anxiety.

5. Adopt Effective Test-Taking Strategies: Develop strategies that will help you approach the test with a clear and organized mindset. Prioritize the questions, read them carefully, and answer the ones you are confident about first. Skip difficult questions and come back to them later. Break down complex problems into smaller parts to make them more manageable.

6. Take Care of Your Physical Health: Prioritize your physical health during the test preparation phase. Get enough sleep, eat nutritious meals, and engage in regular exercise. Taking care of your body will enhance your mental well-being and reduce anxiety.

7. Seek Support: Reach out to supportive friends, family members, or mentors who can provide encouragement and guidance. Consider joining study groups or seeking help from a tutor if you need additional assistance with specific subjects.

By implementing these coping techniques, you can effectively reduce test anxiety and perform at your best. Remember, anxiety is a normal response, but with the right strategies, you can overcome it and achieve your goals.

Chapter 12: Work-Related Anxiety: Coping with Stress and Anxiety in the Workplace

Identifying Work-Related Anxiety Triggers

In today's fast-paced and demanding work environment, it's no surprise that many individuals experience work-related anxiety. This subchapter aims to help individuals identify the triggers that contribute to their work-related anxiety, providing valuable insights and strategies for coping with stress and anxiety in the workplace.

Work-related anxiety can manifest in various ways, such as constant worry about job performance, fear of failure, perfectionism, overwhelming workload, interpersonal conflicts, lack of control, or uncertainty about the future. By identifying the specific triggers that contribute to one's work-related anxiety, individuals can gain a better understanding of their emotional responses and develop effective coping mechanisms.

One way to identify work-related anxiety triggers is through self-reflection and introspection. Taking the time to reflect on one's thoughts, feelings, and physical sensations during stressful work situations can help pinpoint the specific triggers. It can be helpful to keep a journal or make notes whenever anxiety arises, documenting the circumstances and any patterns that emerge.

Another valuable tool for identifying work-related anxiety triggers is seeking feedback from trusted colleagues or supervisors. Often, others can provide valuable insights into patterns of behavior or situations that consistently lead to anxiety. This external perspective can shed light on blind spots or areas for growth that individuals may not have considered on their own.

Additionally, it can be beneficial to explore the underlying beliefs and thoughts that contribute to work-related anxiety. This can be done through therapy, self-help books, or online resources. Challenging and reframing negative or irrational thoughts can help individuals develop a more balanced and realistic perspective, reducing anxiety triggers.

Once work-related anxiety triggers are identified, it becomes easier to develop effective coping strategies. This may include techniques such as deep breathing exercises, mindfulness meditation, setting boundaries, time management, seeking support from colleagues or supervisors, or engaging in stress-reducing activities outside of work.

By understanding their work-related anxiety triggers, individuals can take proactive steps towards managing their stress and anxiety in the workplace. This subchapter provides the tools and insights needed to identify these triggers and develop personalized strategies for coping effectively, ultimately leading to a healthier and more fulfilling work experience.

Strategies for Managing Stress at Work

Introduction:

Work-related anxiety and stress can be overwhelming and detrimental to both our mental and physical well-being. However, there are strategies that can help us cope with and manage stress in the workplace. This subchapter explores various techniques that can be employed to alleviate work-related anxiety and promote a healthier work environment.

1. Identify and Understand Triggers:

The first step in managing work-related stress is to identify the specific triggers that cause anxiety. Whether it's excessive workload, lack of control, or difficult colleagues, understanding these triggers enables us to develop appropriate coping mechanisms.

2. Time Management:

Effective time management plays a crucial role in reducing work-related stress. Prioritize tasks, set realistic deadlines, and break larger projects into smaller manageable chunks. By organizing our time effectively, we can prevent overwhelming workloads and create a sense of control.

3. Establish Boundaries:

Creating boundaries between work and personal life is essential for managing stress. Avoid taking work home whenever possible, and set aside time for relaxation and self-care. By establishing clear boundaries, we can protect our mental well-being and maintain a healthy work-life balance.

4. Practice Stress-Relief Techniques:

Engaging in regular stress-relief techniques can significantly reduce work-related anxiety. Deep breathing exercises, meditation, and physical activities like yoga or walking can help alleviate stress and promote relaxation. Finding a technique that suits our individual needs can make a significant difference in managing work-related stress.

5. Seek Support:

Don't hesitate to seek support from colleagues, friends, or family members. Sharing concerns and experiences with trusted individuals can provide emotional support and offer valuable advice. Additionally, consider talking to a mental health professional who specializes in work-related stress.

6. Effective Communication:

Clear and open communication with colleagues and superiors is crucial for managing work-related stress. Express concerns and boundaries assertively, seek clarification when needed, and address conflicts proactively. Effective communication fosters a healthier work environment and reduces anxiety levels.

7. Take Regular Breaks:

Taking regular breaks throughout the workday is essential for maintaining productivity and managing stress. Use break times to engage in activities that promote relaxation, such as stretching, listening to music, or engaging in a hobby. Stepping away from work for a few minutes can rejuvenate our minds and improve focus.

Conclusion:

While work-related stress is common, it doesn't have to control our lives. By implementing these strategies, we can effectively manage stress in the workplace and create a healthier and more fulfilling work environment. Remember, prioritizing self-care and seeking support are vital components of managing work-related anxiety.

Establishing Healthy Work-Life Balance

In today's fast-paced and demanding world, achieving a healthy work-life balance has become increasingly challenging. The constant pressure to excel in our careers often leads to neglecting our personal lives, resulting in chronic worry and anxiety. This subchapter aims to guide individuals from various backgrounds, including those dealing with social anxiety, panic disorder, generalized anxiety disorder, performance anxiety, health anxiety, post-traumatic stress disorder (PTSD), obsessive-compulsive disorder (OCD), separation anxiety, test anxiety, and work-related anxiety, on how to establish and maintain a healthy work-life balance.

Recognizing the importance of balance is the first step towards a healthier and happier life. By acknowledging that our well-being depends on both our professional and personal lives, we can start making conscious efforts to create equilibrium between the two. This subchapter will provide practical strategies and tips to help individuals strike a balance that works for them.

One of the key aspects of establishing a healthy work-life balance is setting boundaries. Learning to say no to extra work hours or unnecessary commitments can greatly reduce stress and anxiety. Additionally, creating a schedule that allows for dedicated time for both work and personal activities is crucial. This subchapter will delve into effective time management techniques that can help individuals prioritize their tasks and ensure they allocate sufficient time to relax and engage in activities they enjoy.

Moreover, this subchapter will explore the importance of self-care in maintaining a healthy work-life balance. It will emphasize the significance of regular exercise, proper nutrition, and quality sleep in managing anxiety and promoting overall well-being. Additionally, it will highlight the importance of incorporating relaxation techniques such as mindfulness, meditation, and deep breathing exercises into daily routines.

Lastly, this subchapter will address the importance of seeking support and maintaining open communication in the workplace. It will provide guidance on how to effectively communicate with supervisors or colleagues about work-related stressors and anxieties, as well as explore the benefits of seeking professional help when needed.

By implementing the strategies and tips outlined in this subchapter, individuals can break free from the cycle of chronic worry and anxiety, and establish a healthy work-life balance that allows for personal growth, happiness, and success in all areas of life.

Chapter 13: Maintaining Long-Term Anxiety Relief

Creating a Personalized Anxiety Management Plan

Anxiety can be a challenging and overwhelming experience, affecting various aspects of our lives. Whether you are struggling with social anxiety, panic disorder, generalized anxiety disorder, performance anxiety, health anxiety, post-traumatic stress disorder (PTSD), obsessive-compulsive disorder (OCD), separation anxiety, test anxiety, or work-related anxiety, developing a personalized anxiety management plan can help you regain control and find relief.

1. Understanding Your Anxiety: Begin by educating yourself about your specific anxiety condition. Learn about its symptoms, triggers, and underlying causes. This knowledge will empower you to better manage and cope with your anxiety.

2. Seek Professional Help: Consider reaching out to a mental health professional who specializes in your specific anxiety disorder. They can provide an accurate diagnosis and offer evidence-based treatments such as therapy or medication.

3. Identify Triggers: Take note of situations, thoughts, or events that tend to trigger your anxiety. This could be public speaking, certain social situations, health concerns, or work-related stress. Identifying triggers will allow you to develop strategies to manage them effectively.

4. Develop Coping Strategies: Experiment with various coping strategies to find what works best for you. This may include deep breathing exercises, mindfulness meditation, progressive muscle relaxation, journaling, or engaging in activities that bring you joy and relaxation.

5. Create a Support System: Reach out to trusted friends, family members, or support groups who can offer understanding and encouragement. Sharing your experiences with others who have similar challenges can be immensely helpful.

6. Practice Self-Care: Prioritize self-care activities that promote overall well-being. This includes getting enough sleep, maintaining a balanced diet, engaging in regular physical exercise, and incorporating relaxation techniques into your daily routine.

7. Challenge Negative Thoughts: Anxiety often stems from negative and irrational thinking patterns. Learn to identify and challenge these thoughts by questioning their validity and replacing them with more realistic and positive ones.

8. Gradual Exposure: If your anxiety is related to specific situations or fears, consider gradually exposing yourself to them in a controlled and supportive manner. This process, known as exposure therapy, can help desensitize you to the triggers and reduce anxiety over time.

9. Set Realistic Goals: Break down your anxiety management plan into small, achievable goals. Celebrate each milestone reached, as this will boost your confidence and motivation to continue your progress.

10. Practice Patience and Persistence: Overcoming anxiety takes time and effort. Be patient with yourself and remember that setbacks are a natural part of the process. Stay committed to your anxiety management plan and believe in your ability to break free from chronic worry.

By creating a personalized anxiety management plan, you can take proactive steps towards taming your anxiety and reclaiming control over your life. Remember, you are not alone in this journey, and with the right strategies and support, you can overcome anxiety and live a fulfilling life.

Building a Support Network

One of the most powerful tools in overcoming chronic worry and anxiety is building a strong support network. Surrounding yourself with a supportive community can provide comfort, guidance, and encouragement as you navigate the challenges of various anxiety disorders. In this chapter, we will explore the importance of building a support network and provide practical tips for cultivating these vital relationships.

Social Anxiety: Dealing with anxiety in social situations

For individuals struggling with social anxiety, it can be especially helpful to connect with others who understand the unique challenges they face. By joining support groups or seeking therapy, individuals can share experiences, gain insights, and practice social skills in a safe environment. Building connections with understanding friends and loved ones can also provide a solid support system.

Panic Disorder: Understanding and managing panic attacks

When panic attacks strike, having a support network in place is crucial. Loved ones who are familiar with the symptoms and triggers can offer reassurance and help implement coping strategies. Additionally, participating in support groups can provide a sense of belonging and the opportunity to learn from others who have successfully managed their panic disorder.

Generalized Anxiety Disorder: Coping with chronic worry and anxiety

Managing chronic worry is a complex task, but it becomes more manageable with the support of others. Loved ones can offer a listening ear and provide perspective when anxiety feels overwhelming. Seeking therapy or joining support groups allows individuals to connect with others who share similar experiences and learn coping strategies from those who have successfully managed their generalized anxiety disorder.

Performance Anxiety: Overcoming anxiety related to public speaking or performing

Performance anxiety can be debilitating, but a supportive network can help individuals overcome their fears. Friends or family members can offer encouragement and provide constructive feedback. Joining public speaking or performing arts groups allows individuals to practice in a supportive environment and gain confidence over time.

Health Anxiety: Addressing excessive worry about health conditions

Building a support network is particularly important for individuals struggling with health anxiety. Trusted healthcare professionals can provide accurate information and help individuals develop a more balanced perspective. Connecting with others who have faced similar fears can offer reassurance and guidance.

In conclusion, building a support network is a vital step in breaking free from chronic worry and anxiety. Whether it is through therapy, support groups, or connecting with understanding friends and loved ones, a strong support network can provide comfort, guidance, and encouragement. By surrounding yourself with individuals who understand your unique challenges, you can gain valuable insights and develop effective coping strategies. Remember, you are not alone in your journey towards taming anxiety – reach out and build your support network today.

Preventing Relapse and Sustaining Progress

In the journey to breaking free from chronic worry and taming generalized anxiety, it is not enough to simply manage symptoms in the present moment. It is equally important to prevent relapse and sustain the progress made. This subchapter provides valuable insights and strategies for individuals struggling with various anxiety disorders, including social anxiety, panic disorder, generalized anxiety disorder, performance anxiety, health anxiety, post-traumatic stress disorder (PTSD), obsessive-compulsive disorder (OCD), separation anxiety, test anxiety, and work-related anxiety.

Relapse prevention starts by understanding the underlying causes and triggers of anxiety. By identifying these factors, individuals can develop personalized strategies to cope with and prevent the recurrence of anxiety symptoms. This could involve creating a supportive environment, establishing healthy lifestyle habits, and engaging in stress-reducing activities such as exercise, mindfulness, and relaxation techniques.

Support networks play a crucial role in maintaining progress. Surrounding yourself with understanding and supportive individuals can provide a safety net during challenging times. Seeking support from friends, family, or support groups can offer a sense of validation, encouragement, and guidance. Additionally, professional help, such as therapy or counseling, can equip individuals with coping mechanisms and tools to cope with anxiety effectively.

Learning and practicing effective anxiety management techniques is essential for long-term success. These techniques can include cognitive-behavioral therapy (CBT), exposure therapy, and relaxation exercises. By challenging negative thought patterns, gradually facing fears, and incorporating relaxation practices into daily routines, individuals can reduce anxiety symptoms and prevent relapse.

Maintaining progress also requires self-care and self-compassion. Taking care of physical and emotional well-being is vital in managing anxiety. This may involve practicing good sleep hygiene, maintaining a balanced diet, engaging in hobbies and activities that bring joy, and setting realistic goals. By prioritizing self-care, individuals can build resilience, reduce stress, and prevent anxiety from taking over their lives.

Lastly, it is essential to remember that progress is not always linear. Setbacks may occur, and it is crucial to remain patient and persistent. Embracing setbacks as opportunities for growth and learning can help individuals bounce back stronger and continue their journey towards breaking free from chronic worry.

In conclusion, preventing relapse and sustaining progress is a vital component of overcoming anxiety disorders. By understanding the causes and triggers, building a support network, practicing effective anxiety management techniques, prioritizing self-care, and embracing setbacks, individuals can maintain their progress and lead fulfilling lives with reduced anxiety.

Chapter 14: Conclusion: Embracing a Life Free from Chronic Worry

In this final chapter, we have embarked on a journey together to break free from chronic worry and tame generalized anxiety. We have explored various aspects of anxiety and provided practical strategies to help you manage and overcome it. As we come to the end of this book, let us reflect on the progress we have made and the possibilities that lie ahead.

For those struggling with social anxiety, we have discussed techniques to navigate social situations with confidence. By understanding the underlying causes of your anxiety and challenging negative thoughts, you can gradually embrace social interactions and build meaningful connections.

Panic disorder can be debilitating, but by recognizing the signs of panic attacks and implementing relaxation techniques, you can regain control over your body and mind. Remember, panic attacks are temporary, and you have the power to overcome them.

Generalized anxiety disorder often leads to chronic worry. By adopting healthy coping mechanisms such as mindfulness, exercise, and seeking support from loved ones, you can learn to manage your worries and prevent them from controlling your life.

Performance anxiety can be crippling, whether it's related to public speaking or performing. We have provided strategies to help you overcome this anxiety, such as visualization, deep breathing exercises, and gradual exposure to the feared situation. With practice, you can develop the confidence to shine on stage or in any public setting.

Health anxiety can consume your thoughts and impact your well-being. By distinguishing between normal concern and excessive worry, seeking professional help when needed, and practicing self-care, you can regain peace of mind and focus on living a healthy life.

Post-traumatic stress disorder (PTSD) can be a result of traumatic experiences. We have explored techniques such as cognitive restructuring, exposure therapy, and self-compassion to help you manage the anxiety stemming from these events. Remember, healing takes time, and you are not alone on this journey.

Obsessive-compulsive disorder (OCD) can be characterized by intrusive thoughts and rituals. By challenging the irrational beliefs driving these behaviors and implementing cognitive-behavioral techniques, you can alleviate the anxiety associated with OCD and regain control over your life.

Separation anxiety can be distressing, especially when it comes to being apart from loved ones. By developing healthy coping mechanisms, maintaining open communication, and seeking professional guidance, you can overcome the anxiety and enjoy fulfilling relationships while also fostering independence.

Test anxiety can hinder academic success, but with preparation, positive self-talk, and relaxation techniques, you can manage anxiety during exams and assessments. Remember, your worth is not determined by a single test.

Work-related anxiety is prevalent in today's society, but by setting boundaries, practicing self-care, and seeking support from colleagues and mentors, you can cope with stress and anxiety in the workplace. Remember, your well-being should always be a priority.

As we conclude this book, I encourage you to embrace these strategies, practice self-compassion, and seek professional help when needed. Remember, overcoming chronic worry is a journey, and it is never too late to start. By implementing these tools, you can create a life free from the shackles of anxiety and embrace a future filled with hope, peace, and fulfillment.